Simply Opera

21 Selections from the Greatest Operas

Arranged by Tom Gerou

Simply Opera is a collection of arias, dances, choruses, interludes and overtures from famous operas. These selections have been carefully arranged by Tom Gerou for Easy Piano, making them accessible to pianists of all ages. Phrase markings, articulations, fingering, pedaling and dynamics have been included to aid with interpretation, and a large print size makes the notation easy to read.

Opera has been an important part of Western culture for more than 400 years, fusing music with acting and dancing, and creating a heightened theatrical experience for people around the world. Mozart, Verdi, and Puccini were just some of the many great composers who favored writing operas over other musical genres. Their masterful melodies became very popular among musicians and audiences.

Music from opera is a pleasure to play on the piano. With opera's *bel canto* ("beautiful singing") style, melodies soar. With its orchestral color, accompaniments dance and sparkle. Additionally, opera music transports its listeners to far-away places and distant times, like 19th-century Japan or even ancient Rome. Opera music also covers the entire spectrum of human emotions—arias can be tender, overtures can be noble, and interludes can be deeply spiritual. For these reasons and many more, the following pages are exciting to explore.

After all, this is *Simply Opera!*

D1567159

Contents

Piangeró la sorte mia

(from *Giulio Cesare*)

George Frideric Handel
Arranged by Tom Gerou

La donna è mobile

(from *Rigoletto*)

Giuseppe Verdi
Arranged by Tom Gerou

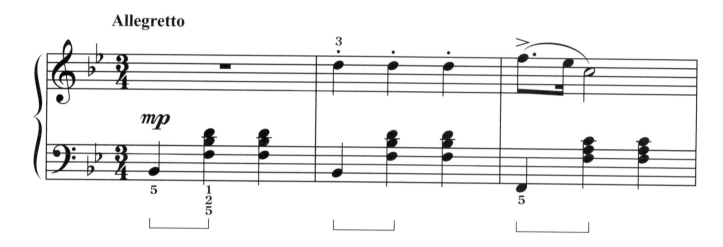

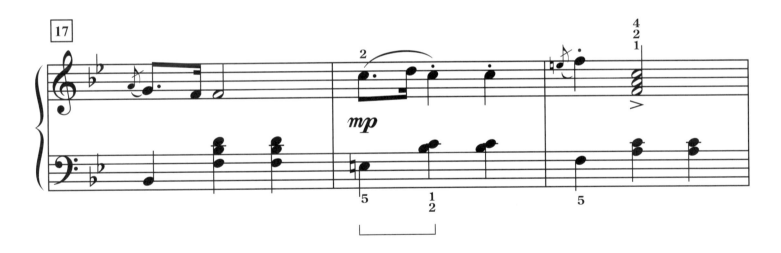

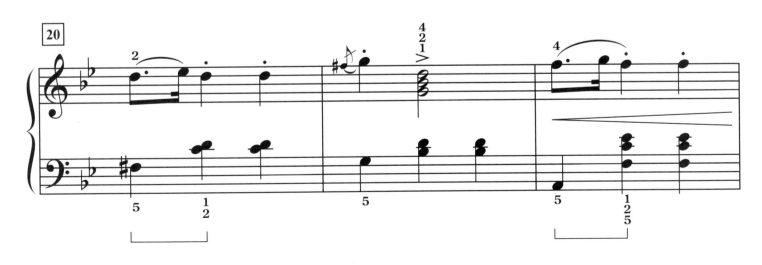

Barcarolle
(from *Tales of Hoffmann*)

Jacques Offenbach
Arranged by Tom Gerou

Moderato

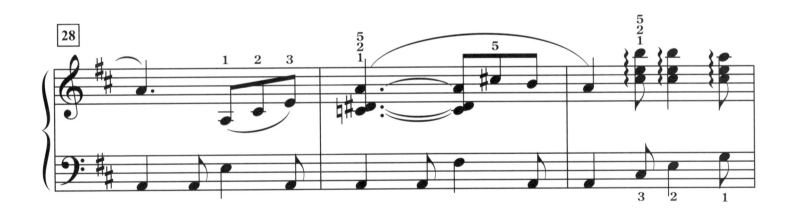

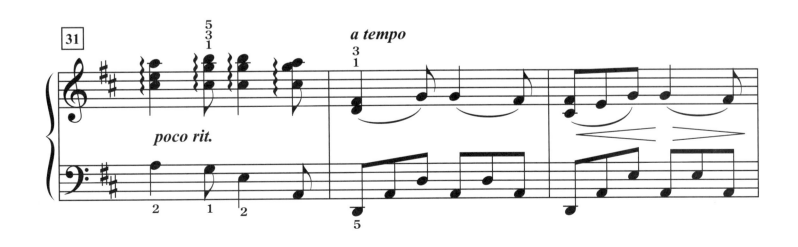

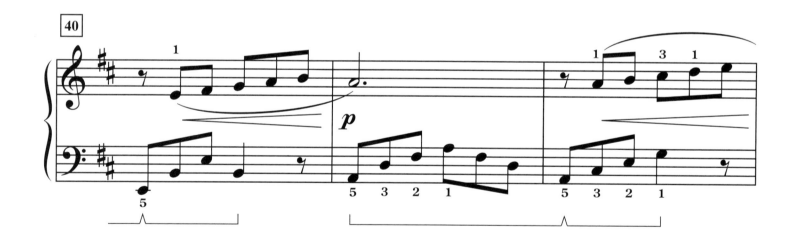

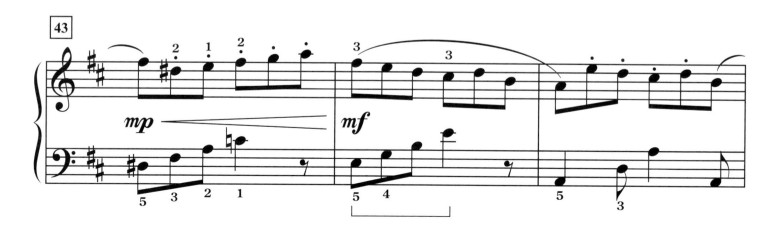

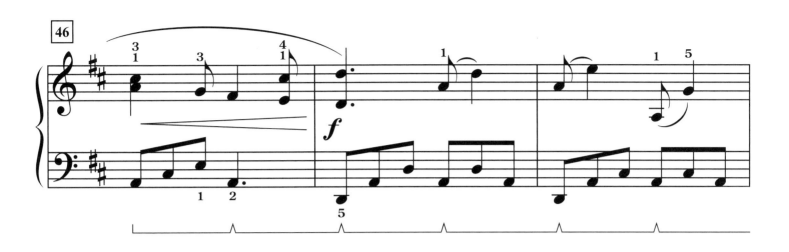

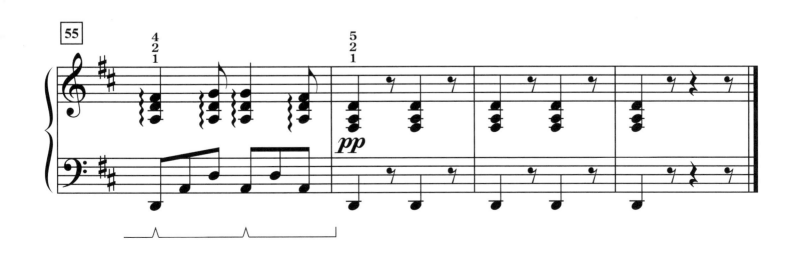

Flower Duet

(from *Lakmé*)

Léo Delibes
Arranged by Tom Gerou

Allegro moderato

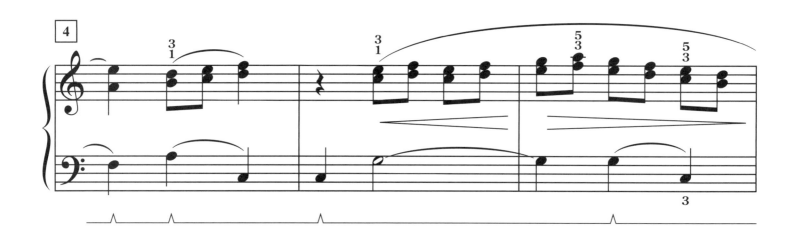

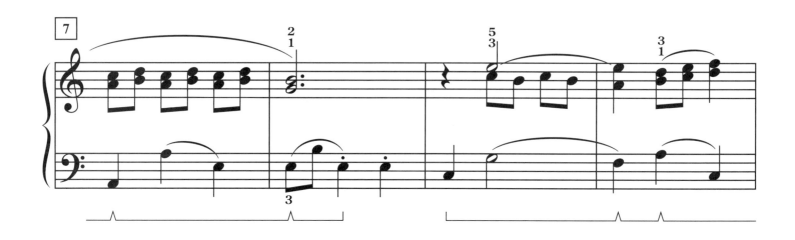

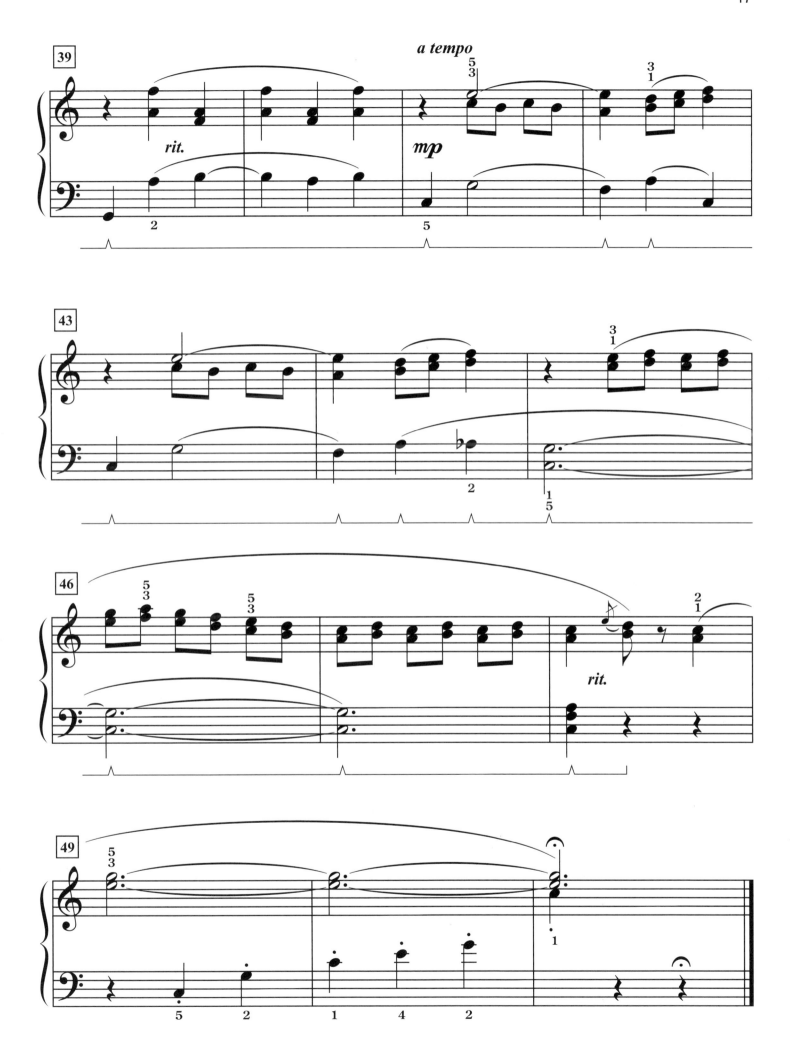

Queen of the Night Aria

(from *The Magic Flute*)

Wolfgang Amadeus Mozart
Arranged by Tom Gerou

Allegro assai

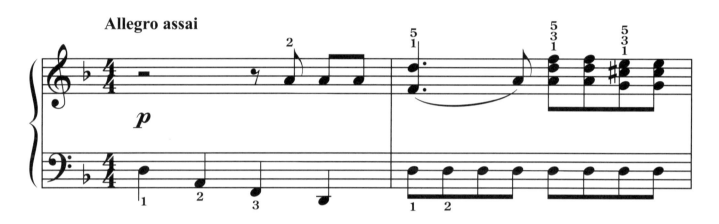

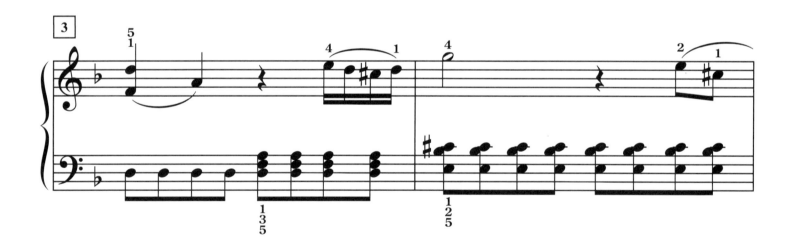

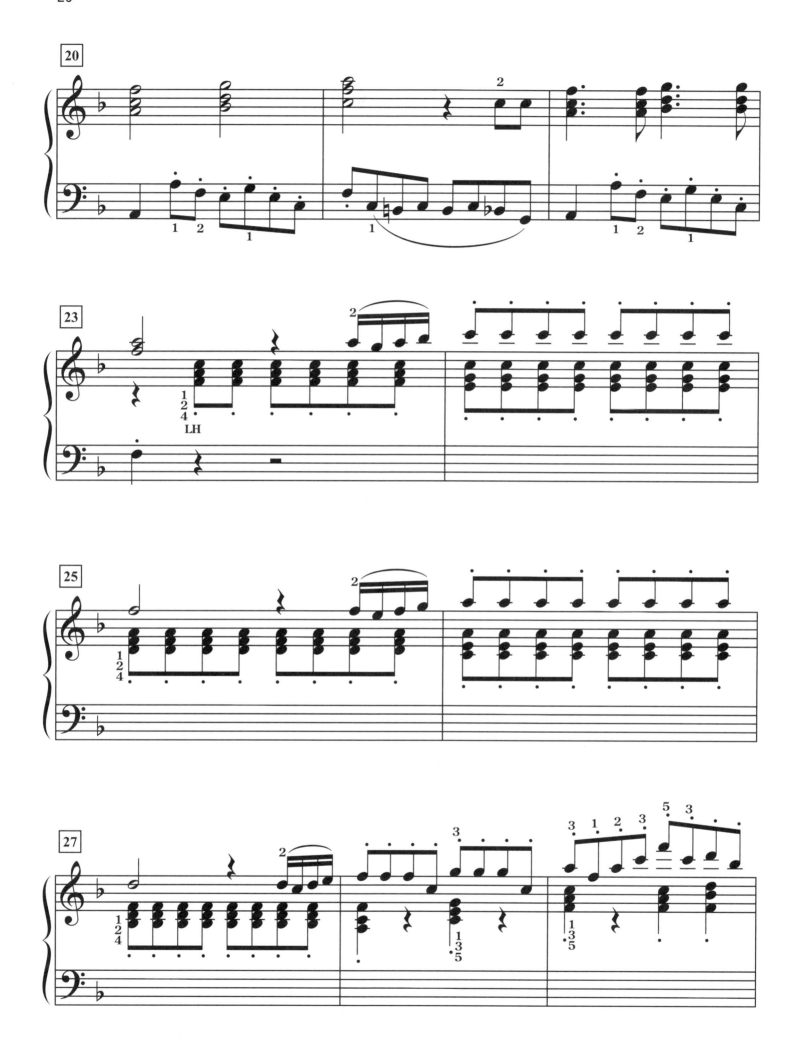

Doretta's Song
(from *La rondine*)

Giacomo Puccini
Arranged by Tom Gerou

Sustained

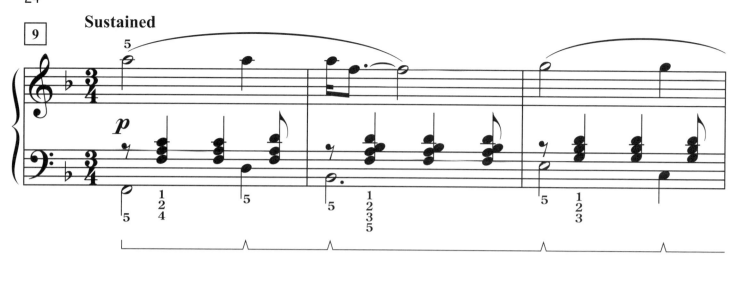

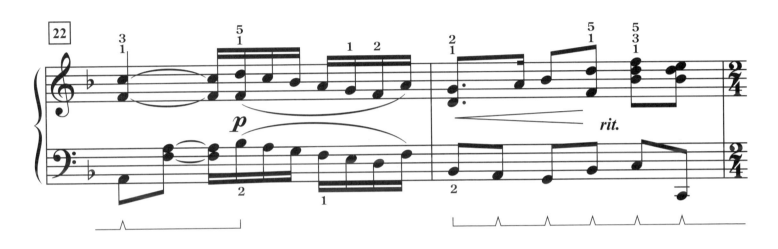

Broadly, sustained

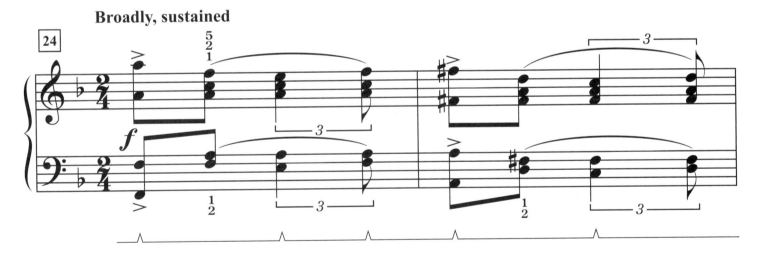

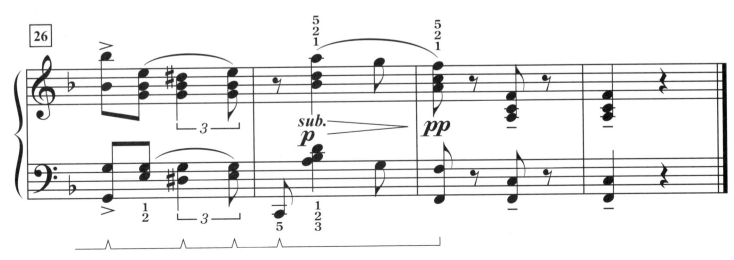

Intermezzo

(from *Cavalleria rusticana*)

Pietro Mascagni
Arranged by Tom Gerou

Connais-tu le pays

(from *Mignon*)

Ambroise Thomas
Arranged by Tom Gerou

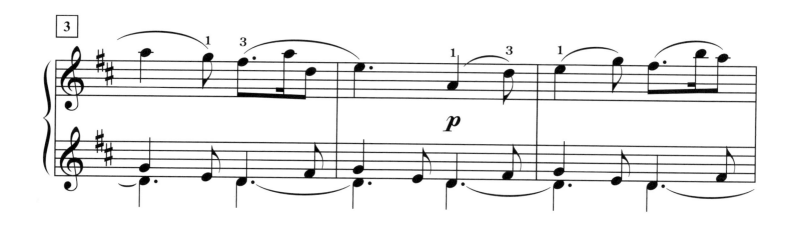

Toreador Song
(from *Carmen*)

Georges Bizet
Arranged by Tom Gerou

Allegro moderato

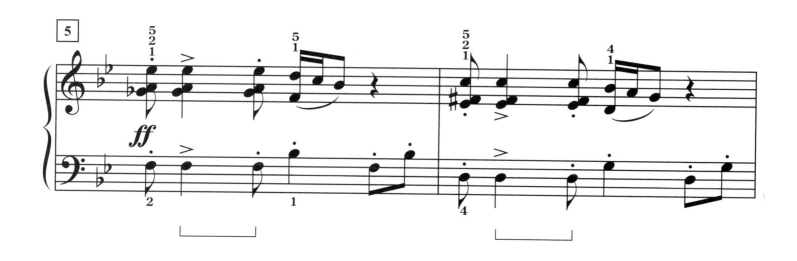

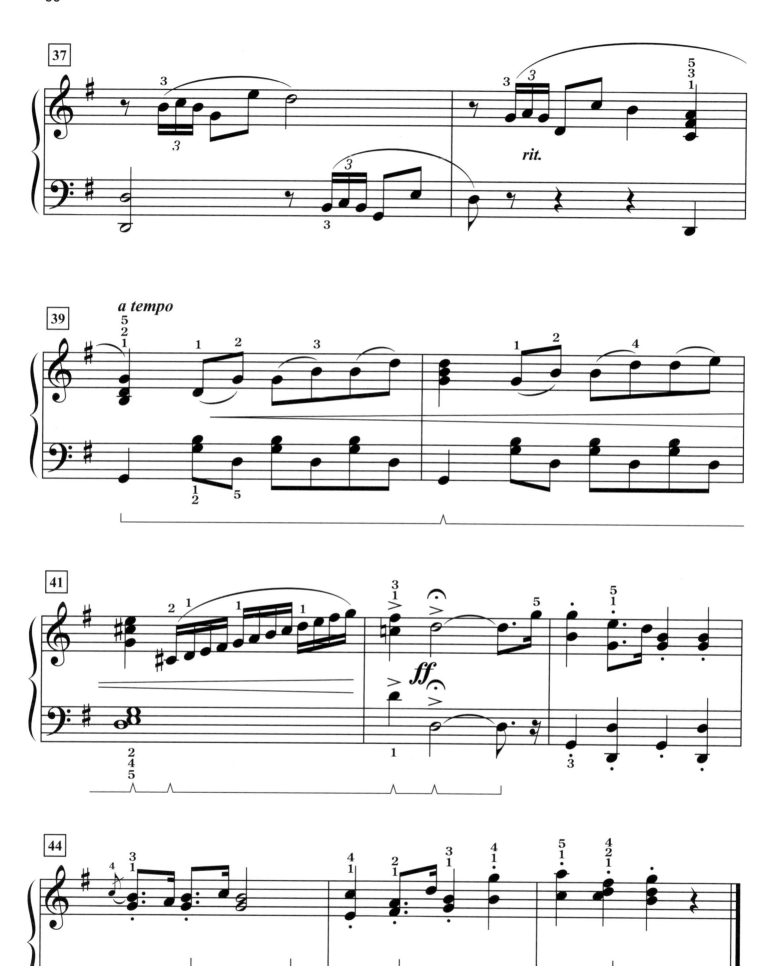

Là ci darem la mano

(from *Don Giovanni*)

Wolfgang Amadeus Mozart
Arranged by Tom Gerou

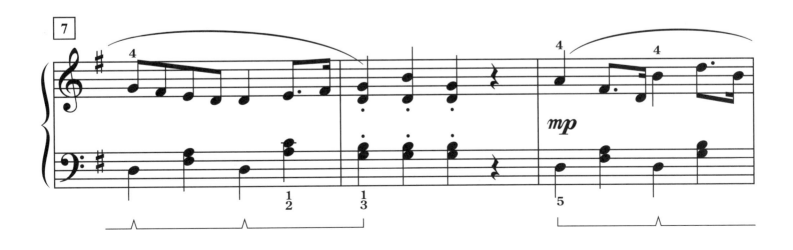

Habanera

(from *Carmen*)

Georges Bizet
Arranged by Tom Gerou

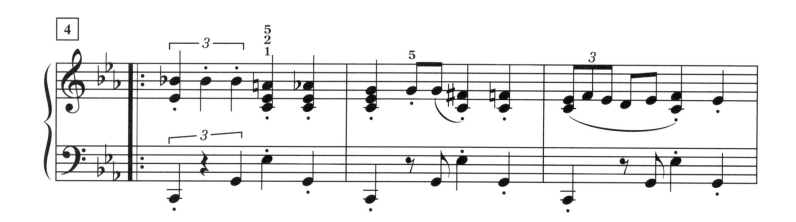

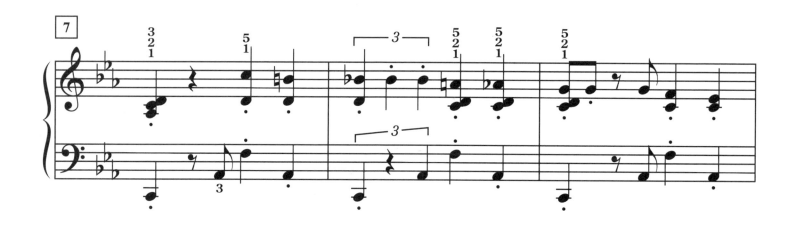

Anvil Chorus
(from *Il trovatore*)

Giuseppe Verdi
Arranged by Tom Gerou

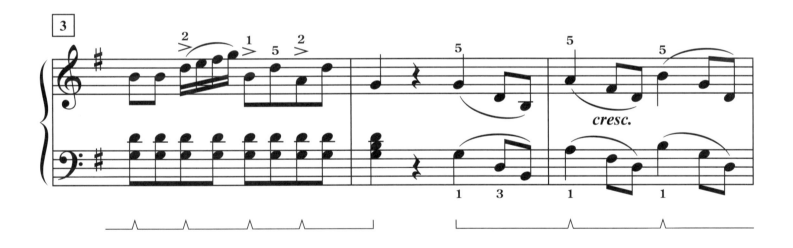

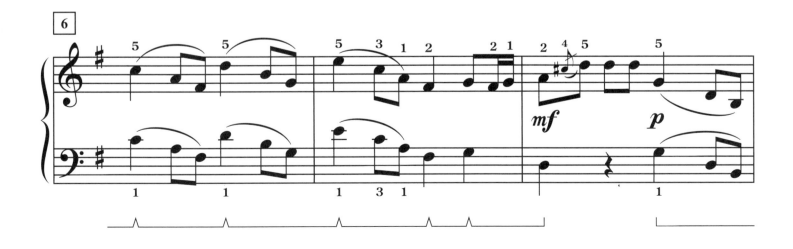

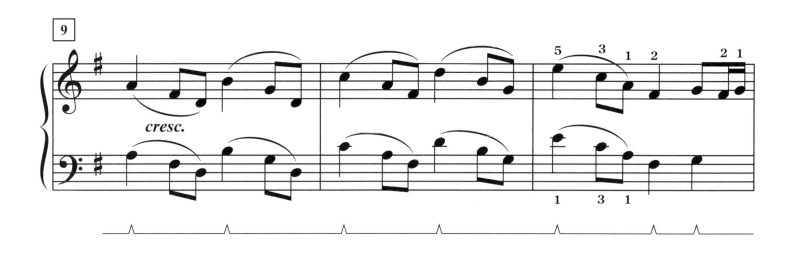

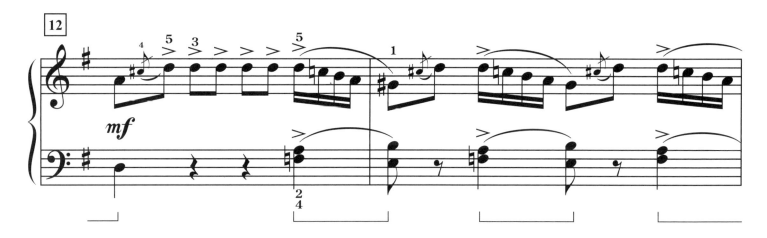

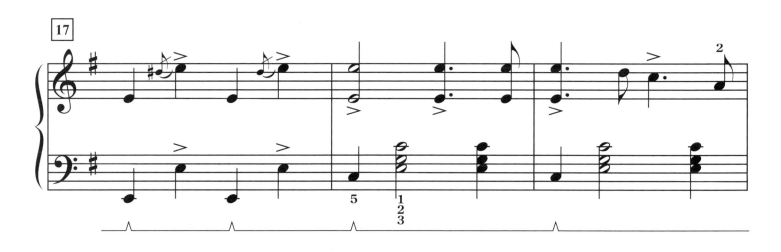

Libiamo
(from *La traviata*)

Giuseppe Verdi
Arranged by Tom Gerou

Allegretto

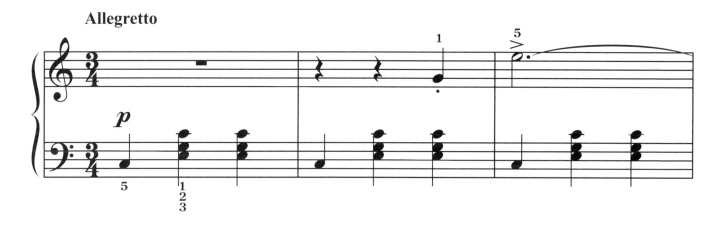

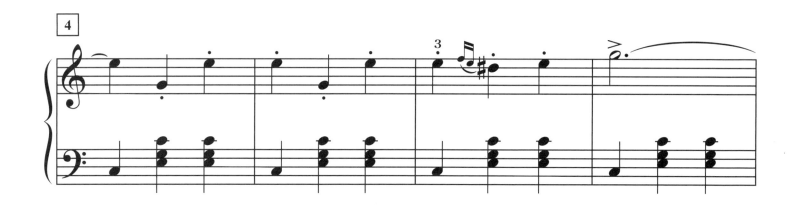

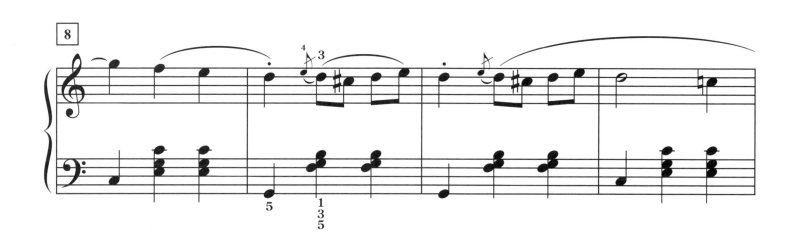

O mio babbino caro

(from *Gianni Schicchi*)

Giacomo Puccini
Arranged by Tom Gerou

Andante, con rubato

55

Musetta's Waltz

(from *La bohème*)

Giacomo Puccini
Arranged by Tom Gerou

Tempo di valse lento

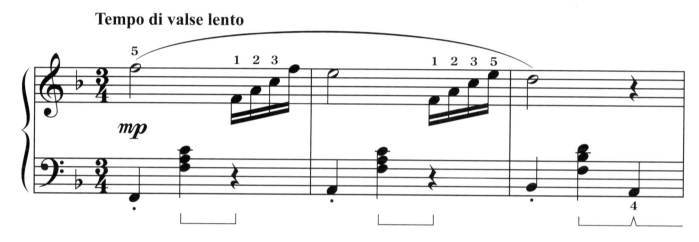

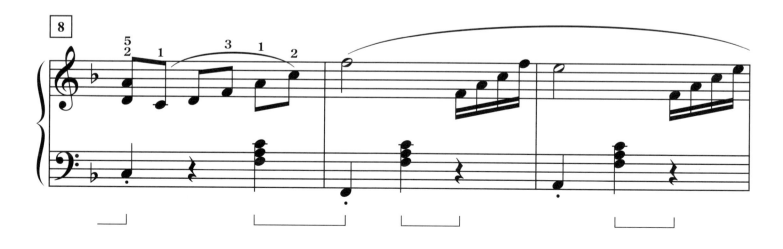

Lascia ch'io pianga

(from *Rinaldo*)

George Frideric Handel
Arranged by Tom Gerou

Un bel dì

(from *Madama Butterfly*)

Giacomo Puccini
Arranged by Tom Gerou

Andante, molto calmo

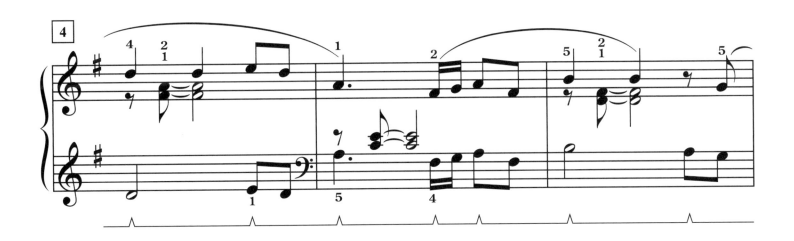

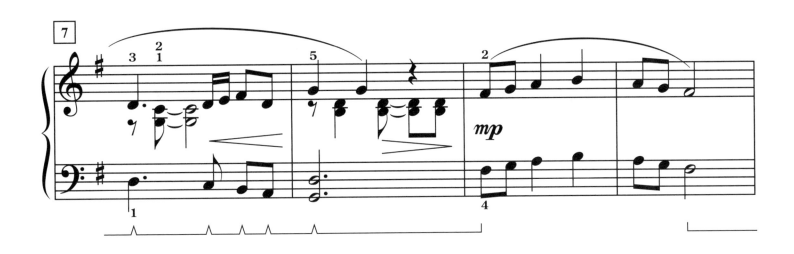

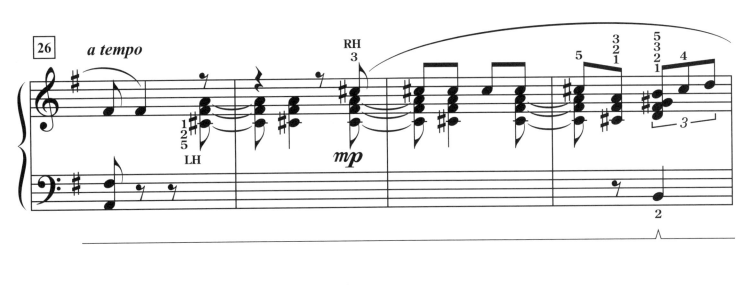

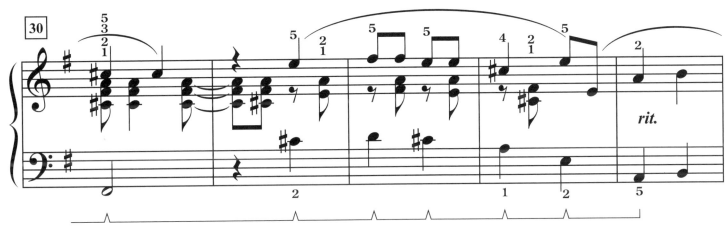

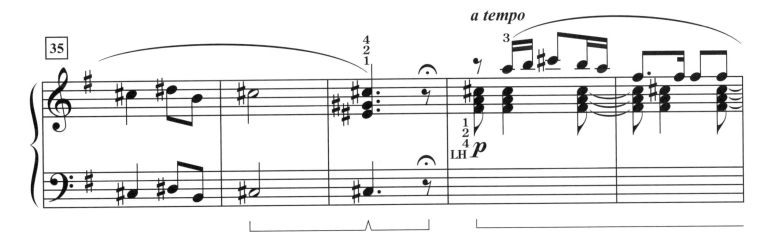

Ebben, ne andrò lontano

(from *La Wally*)

Alfredo Catalani
Arranged by Tom Gerou

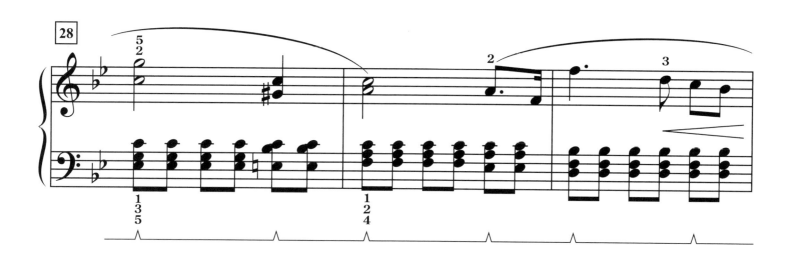

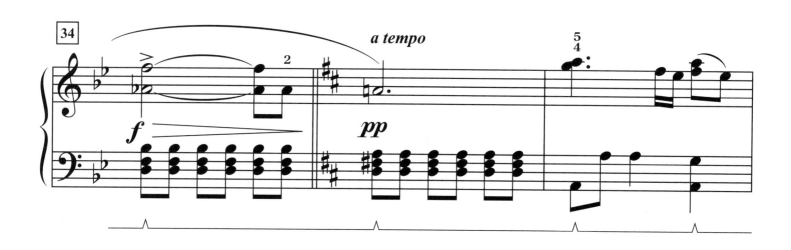

Voi, che sapete

(from *The Marriage of Figaro*)

Wolfgang Amadeus Mozart
Arranged by Tom Gerou

Andante con moto

74

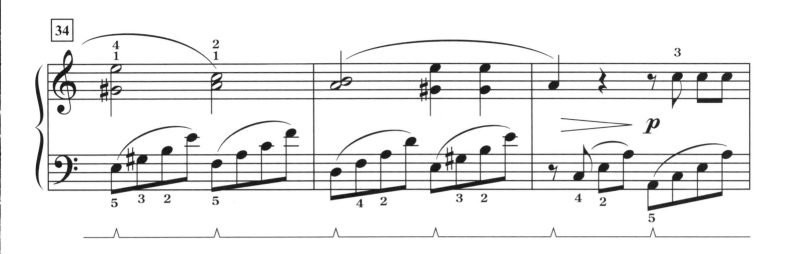

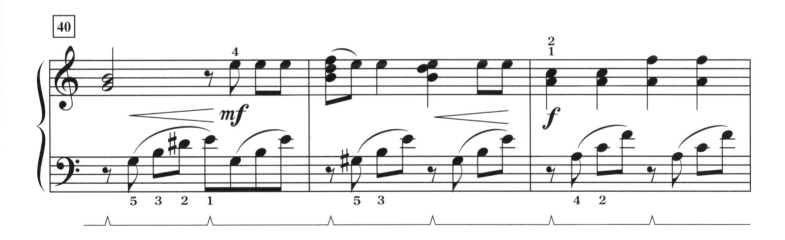

D.C. al Fine

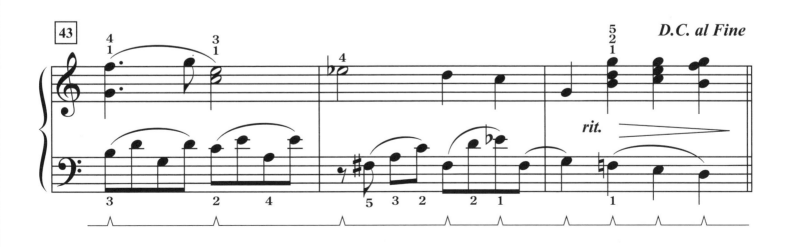

Meditation
(from *Thaïs*)

Jules Massenet
Arranged by Tom Gerou

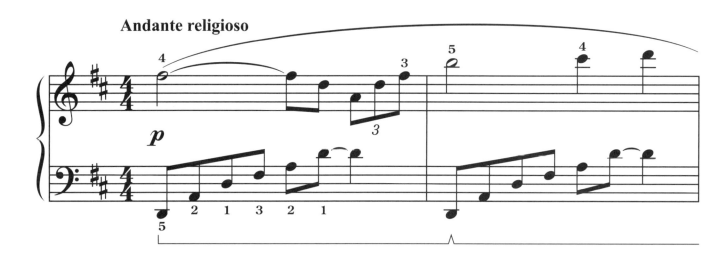

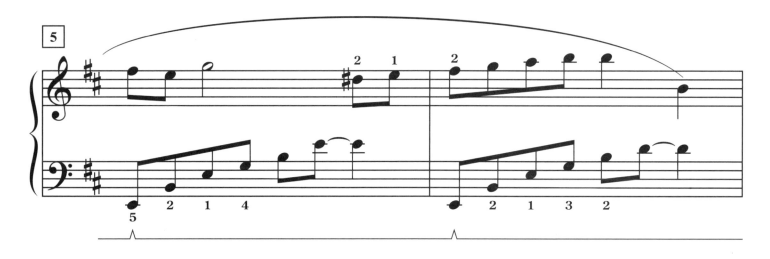

78

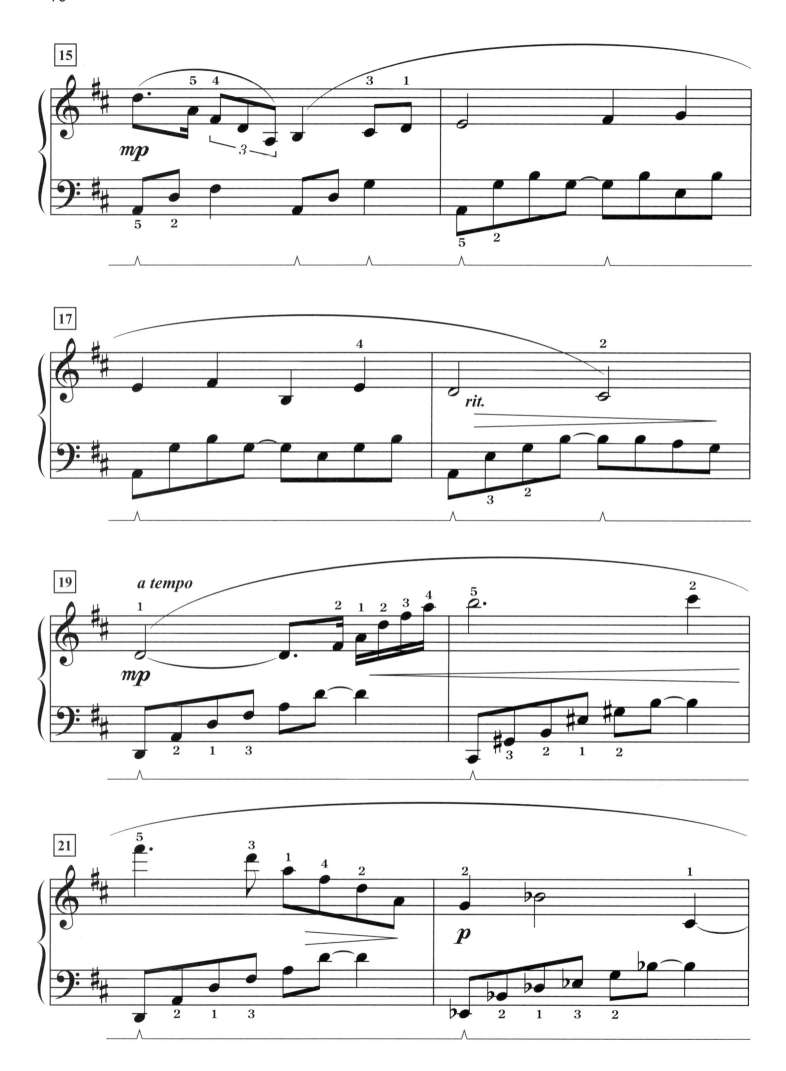

Forse, come la rondine

(from *La rondine*)

Giacomo Puccini
Arranged by Tom Gerou